The Other Shore
A Buddhist training manual
for daily life

Michael Kewley
Dhammachariya Paññadipa

All rights reserved.
Copyright © Michael Kewley 2007

No part of this publication may be reproduced, stored in a retrieval system or transmitted, in any form or by any means, electronic, mechanical, photocopying, recording or otherwise, without prior permission of the publishers.

This book is sold subject to the condition that it shall not by way of trade or otherwise, be lent, re-sold, hired out or otherwise circulated without the publishers prior consent in any form of binding cover other than that in which it is published and without similar condition including this condition being imposed on the subsequent purchaser.

ISBN: 978-1-899417-07-0

Published by:
Panna Dipa Books.
E-mail:
dhammateacher@hotmail.com

Typeset & cover design by
Akaliko.
E-mail:
akaliko@free.fr

The Other Shore

Dedication

For all those who truly want
to reach the other shore.

The Other Shore

*Few men reach the other shore.
Almost all run up and down
This side of the river.*

                        Dhammapada: Verse 85

The Other Shore

Introduction

The Buddha is my inspiration, my role model, my hero! We bumped into each other when I was eighteen years old, and for thirty five years I have ardently followed his path of Love and Awareness, even to the extent spending time as a Buddhist monk in the Theravada tradition.
I was always a disciple!

My reason for following Dhamma was simple, I wanted to be free - to end my suffering, and so I applied myself to each moment with sincerity and I took the training into my life!

Of course, during these thirty five years of training I have established a personal relationship with the Buddha, first seeing him as the traditional super perfect, but sometimes intolerant being as depicted in the scriptures, to my relationship now, to know him as a beautifully complete human being. One who has realised the reality of existence, but more, wanted to share that experience with all beings. I can only see the Buddha with my own heart, but I feel that he must have been a man with an infinite Love and Compassion for others, and although it is not really said in the scriptures, a magnificent sense of humour, for these are the qualities of Love, of Dhamma.

Dhamma is not a religion or a dogma. It is not a set of social and cultural rules to be followed without argument. It is the way to be free. To take responsibility for ones actions, and the consequence of those actions, and to be awake in ones life.

For more than thirty years I have devoted myself to this path, and as a consequence, seen my life open like a flower. To experience fully the consequence of Love, Awareness and Compassion, a life of joy, of celebration and fearlessness.

And so, if you truly want to be free from the conditions that give rise to your suffering, to your unhappiness, you must do the same, you must make the effort, there is no other way!

When you make the effort you will receive the result of that effort. When you make no effort, you will receive the result of making no effort. The rest is for you to decide.

> I offer you my best wishes
> for your own spiritual journey.
>
> May all beings be happy

Michael Kewley
Augé, France
February 2007

CONTENTS

PART 1
The Spiritual Life

PART 2
Finding the Way

PART 3
Meditation and Love

PART 4
Crossing the River

PART 5
Daily Inspirations

The Other Shore

Part 1

The Spiritual Life

The Other Shore

Cease to do evil,
Learn to do good,
Purify your own mind.
This is the teaching of all the Buddhas.

Dhammapada: Verse 183

The Other Shore

The Spiritual Life
The opening of the wisdom eye

According to the traditional Buddhist story, the man who became enlightened and so earned the title 'Buddha', was born as an ordinary human being in a small country in the northern part of what is now India. He was the son of a king and so carried the social position of 'prince'. His name was Siddhartha Gotama.

His life in the palace was truly luxurious, and prince Siddhartha always had everything that he wished for. He could rest just when he wanted, play just when he wanted, eat only the best food and wear the finest clothes, just when he wanted, play sports and sleep, just when he wanted to. He was surrounded by caring and loving people and had a strong and healthy body. At the age of sixteen he was married to his beautiful cousin, the princess Yashodhara, and was destined to become a great king like his father.

However, Siddhartha was an intelligent and reflective young man, and without a consideration for the consequences, he began to question fundamental assumptions about his life. As a prince he always had every kind of pleasure and sense gratification that he desired. Just a snap of the fingers and he could have whatever he wanted, but in reality, it was never enough. This meal only carried him through to his next meal, this sleep only carried him through to the next sleep. This sexual satisfaction only carried him through to the next sexual satisfaction, and so on, and so on. However hard he tried, he could never be completely satisfied by fulfilling his desires, and so always was in the position of wanting more. Of looking for the next thing to bring the sense of happiness into his life.

The happiness that arrived though was always transient and could never be guaranteed simply by following an action that had been successful in the past. He began to realise that everything he had, everything he thought he owned or was his, could be taken away from him at any moment and that his own life, like the life of everyone else, was fragile and impossible to protect from the natural vicissitudes that affect everyone. That no matter how socially high his princely status was, in his real life as a fellow human being, he was in exactly the same position as everyone else in the world. No matter what he could buy with his enormous wealth, and what physical comforts could be offered to him, he would never be completely satisfied, and he would still have to meet old age, sickness and death. These it seemed, were inescapable.

So now arose the most disturbing questions of all, the questions that kept away his sleep at night, and his peace during the day. The questions he had posed to the wisest and most religious men in his fathers kingdom, and all without an inspiring or suitable reply.

What is the purpose of life? Why are we born, when life only takes us to death, and often with much pain and despair? Why is happiness so elusive and always so short lived? What is the point of it all?

These thoughts became a daily reflection for the young prince, and he was no longer able to turn away from them. Disturbed and frustrated by the realities of life, prince Siddhartha, heir to the Sakyan kingdom, at the age of twenty nine, and on the day of the birth of his son, secretly crept away from the palace to find a path that would show him the way to peace and contentment and give real understanding as to the nature of life.

Although the early life of prince Siddhartha happened in country far away from Europe almost two thousand six hundred years ago, it is not really so different from our life now, living with every kind of modern convenience, in the early twenty first century.

Our homes are bombarded by images from the television and magazines that tell us how celebrities live. How singers and actors are the examples of life that we need to follow. Of how we must be young, beautiful and slim, and like them to be happy.

That we need to live in superbly furnished homes and apartments, and eat incredibly healthy, yet ready made and instant meals, to be happy. That we need to take exotic holidays and stay in exclusive hotels and resorts, to be happy.

Our society with its traditional forms of conditioning tells us that the way to happiness is through education, marriage, children and career. Unfortunately the real experience of our own life, tells us all something different. Even when we have, or have done what we are told to do, even when we have fulfilled the social, economic and religious conditions for happiness, we still find that a real and satisfying happiness is as elusive for us as it was for prince Siddhartha. Even when we repeat our special and private formulas of romance, sex and more hard work, we find exactly as prince Siddhartha did, they cannot be guaranteed to work in our favour.

If we are brave enough to reflect honestly upon the unsatisfactory and illusive nature of happiness, and using the reality of our own personal experience in life, we can be inspired to become true spiritual seekers.

The Seeker

The seeker is the one who wants to know, and who in the end, is not afraid of the truth. The seeker is the one who will make the effort to understand, harmonise and flow with the truth and not try to bend or manipulate it to suit himself, but to peacefully accept the reality of each moment.

True seekers are rare, because the path is long, very often boring and frustrating and filled with conditions that are perceived as obstacles. However, these obstacles are in fact, the very gateways to our liberation. With the right effort and determination we can transcend these obstacles and use them to our advantage. It is said like this:

> Without our suffering,
> how could we overcome our suffering?

Our difficulties then, are only obstacles if we see them that way. If we look for a reason to stop our spiritual practice or to justify our laziness.

In reality our path to liberation is right in front of us and is already completely perfect.

The seeker is not very much interested in religion, politics or self glorification, only their own spiritual evolution. The movement from darkness to light, fear to love, ignorance to wisdom. Burning incense and praying to deities can be useful tools to focus the mind, but in reality are not more than that. Neither is claiming membership to one religious or social group or another. No matter how hard we try, these will not help us to end our suffering and unhappiness, or bring peace to ourselves or the world.

> Those who mistake the shadow for the substance
> And the substance for the shadow
> Will never arrive at the reality
> And only follow a false path.

Dhammapada: Verse 11

Upatissa, Kolita and Sañjaya

Upatissa and Kolita were born on the same day in the same part of the country. They became friends in their childhood, and remained that way all their lives. They were both from wealthy Brahmin families and so, like Prince Siddhartha, were able to enjoy all of the pleasures that a privileged life could offer.

One day, in their adolescent years, they went to the local annual festival to be entertained, amazed and delighted by the performers.

When it was the moment to be amazed, they were amazed, when it was the moment to be afraid, they were afraid, when it was the moment to be thrilled they were thrilled! Like every member of the audience they thoroughly enjoyed the show.

As with many Indian festivals, it continued over many days, and so the next day they returned to be further entertained by the acts. This time however, something was different.

The excitement and the enthusiasm of the previous day had paled, and they sat together and looked at the show with confused eyes. Where was the excitement, where was the thrill of the story, where was the joy of being entertained?

On the third day they returned, but now it was clear. The spiritual eye of each had opened, and they could no longer be interested by the emptiness presented to them. Everything here was only a thin veneer of noise and colour, covering the reality of insubstantiality. In that moment there was a flash of illumination as each experienced exactly the same thought:

'Of what use is it to sit here and watch this nonsense? In reality life is passing so quickly that there is not one single moment to waste. One day I, and everything I know, will be gone. Now is the time when I must make the effort to discover and understand the real value and meaning of life.'

Realising this most profound truth, that life is indeed impermanent, they agreed to leave their comfortable existence immediately and train with a teacher who could show them the way to know the highest truths.

They arrived at the camp of Sañjaya, a well known ascetic teacher with many hundreds of disciples, and asked if they could be accepted to train with him. He agreed immediately.

Upatissa and Kolita worked hard with Sañjaya and after a short time both had excelled at the various disciplines taught to them. Now they were ready to go further with their practice and so asked if there was more to learn.

"Ah, no," answered Sañjaya, "This is everything I know."

"Then we must leave you and go continue our search," replied the two friends. "This is not the final truth we are looking for."

They left Sañjaya and decided to go their separate ways in their search for a true teacher. They made a pact, established in their trust and friendship, that whoever found this teacher first would come immediately and fetch the other.

Saying goodbye and wishing each other success, they parted.

Some time later, Upatissa was in the busy town of

Ragagaya when he saw something that deeply touched his heart. Standing at the doorway of a house receiving alms food in his bowl, was a most beautiful and elegant man. Obviously a true spiritual seeker, he accepted what was offered in silence and with gratitude and moved on to the next house.

Upatissa was so impressed by this beautiful comportment, that he discreetly followed this man until he had arrived at the river, sat elegantly under a tree, and ate his small meal. When he had finished and cleaned his bowl, Upatissa approached and spoke.

"Excuse me sir, but will you please tell me who you are and, if you have a teacher, what is his name?"

This spiritual man was no ordinary disciple of a teacher. His name was Assaji, and he was one of the first five beings in the world to arrive at enlightenment through teachings and instructions from the Buddha.

Assaji answered the questions of Upatissa gladly, and explained that he was on his way to join him soon. Upatissa then asked if he could share some of the Buddhas teachings to him.

Assaji humbly answered in the following way.

"Actually I am quite new to this, and if you truly want to hear the teaching of the Buddha, you must go to him. I can only repeat something very simply that may help you. The Buddha has reminded us that in all existence, nothing just happens, and that everything we can know is the consequence of that which preceded it."

When Upatissa heard these words his heart opened and he attained the first level of enlightenment. He thought, 'This is magnificent. Now I must find Kolita to tell him what I have understood, so that we can go to the Buddha together.'

Paying his respects and saying goodbye to Assaji, Upatissa left to find his friend.

When they met some time later, Upatissa was enthusiastic to share what he had understood with his friend and so spoke without hesitation. Kolita listened and also immediately understood the few words given by Assaji. In that moment he too attained the first level of enlightenment.

'Now we must go to the Buddha in person and complete our training with him', they thought, and so they took their first few steps towards the new life that waited for them.

However after a moment, Kolita stopped and spoke to Upatissa.

"Upatissa, we are forgetting our old teacher, Sañjaya, he too would enjoy to hear this teaching so that he may experience the same fruits as us."

"Kolita my friend," replied Upatissa, "You are right, of course. We must go straight there to give him the good news."

And this they did.

Sañjaya was delighted to see his two former disciples returning, but was not happy to hear what they had to say.

"Master," they began, "We have found the perfect teacher and the perfect teaching. You must also come to train with him so that you too can experience what we have already experienced."

"Ah, my friends," replied Sañjaya, "This I cannot do. Look around you. Here I am the master of many disciples, I cannot now become the disciple to a teacher again. It will be too hard for me to loose what I have here. You go, but I must stay"

From love and compassion for their former teacher, Upatissa and Kolita argued for Sañjaya to go with them, but without success. Sañjaya had everything he wanted here, even if it had no value.

Finally they presented one last reason.

"Master, when it is known that a true Buddha has appeared in the world, people will flock to him for his teachings. At that time you will be without students. Please come with us."

"My friends," replied Sañjaya, "Which do you think is more in the world, foolish people or wise people?"

"Foolish people, we suppose," they answered.

"So," continued Sañjaya, "Let the wise people go to the Buddha, and I will keep the foolish ones. In this way I will never be without disciples."

With this answer, and a heavy heart Upatissa and Kolita left Sañjaya for the final time and went to meet the Buddha.

Upatissa and Kolita joined the Buddha and trained with him. Quickly they were fully enlightened and in time became the two chief disciples, known as Sariputta and Moggallana.

> Those who know the substance as the substance
> And the shadow as the shadow
> Arrive at the reality
> And follow the true path.

Dhammapada: Verse 12

Our modern life also is like that of the two young friends, filled with entertainments and distractions. Television, cinema, theatre, restaurants, music. So many different ways to keep us from what is truly valuable. The realisation of truth in our life.

Even the attitude of Sañjaya is not uncommon today, when so many people want fame and popularity at the expense of their personal integrity. Always, if we truly look, we can see that the television, an essential part of almost every home, is only the window for our foolishness and arrogance.

The spiritual life demands that we awaken to reality, no matter how comfortable our sleeping state is.

However, even though we may be able to raise the determination to be free and to transform our life, at the beginning of our spiritual journey, until we know for ourselves, we will need some guidance, some support.

Traditionally the first part of our training begins with a way to live in the world. Not to follow the mind and its desires, but rather to follow the advice of wise people.

Our path then, begins with a simple, yet supremely powerful morality, expressed as:

> Not to do harm to ourselves
> or others through body or speech.

As always, for the genuine seeker of truth, these instructions are only ever guidelines and not a list of rules that one must follow for fear of punishment or retribution from an external agent. The consequence of our actions follows us through our life until it comes to fruition, and we must accept the reality of this.

In short, we are always responsible for what we do or say!

Ultimately, the morality that we cultivate must be a natural morality, arising from a loving and compassionate heart, not something imposed on our life.

When the heart awakens we will come to understand that we do not harm other beings, not because the Buddha said that we should not, but that there is no desire or instinct in the heart to do so. From this position of clarity, at least one aspect of our lives becomes peaceful. We will find also that because harmlessness (Ahimsa) is a natural part of how we live, there is never the need to expound, justify or explain our own personal views of life with the further idea of persuading others that we are right, and they would do well to follow our way.

Each person is responsible for their conduct and how they live. This responsibility is unique and personal, and cannot be assumed or taken on by another, no matter how well intentioned.

> Let us live happily without hating
> Those who hate us.
> Let us be free from hatred
> Amongst those who hate.

Dhammapada: Verse 197

The Teaching of self responsibility

At one time the Buddha visited the small town of Kesaputta in the kingdom of Kosala. The people of this town were known by the common name of Kalama, and were not strangers to visiting holy men.

When they heard that the Buddha had arrived they went eagerly to see him and hear him expound his teachings like so many of the others had done in the past. However the Buddha remained silent until someone asked a question.

"Sir, there are many wandering teachers passing through our town, each one criticising the others, and all expounding their own doctrine. It becomes a real problem for us when we hear so many conflicting teachings, and it is impossible for us to know which one to follow. Here you are silent, but we ask you to speak. Please advise us as to how we can know which teaching we should follow."

The Buddha then spoke and gave the teaching of self responsibility, which appears to be unique in the history of religion.

"My friends," began the Buddha, "You are right to question and reflect upon the teachings you have heard, and it is understandable that you have doubt and apprehension, but my teaching to you is simple, and I ask you not to accept it or reject it, but only to consider it.

Kalamas, do not be impressed by reports you have heard, or by tradition or rumour. Neither be impressed by the authority of someone who can speak of religious texts, or who can argue and present a case in favour of, or against something. Do not even be impressed by the ones who call themselves 'Buddha' and claim enlightenment, rather listen to your own heart.

This is important to understand.

Only when you know from your heart that something is good should you follow it, and the moment you know that something is not good should you abandon it. The truly beneficial life is established in goodness, not religious piety, and the responsibility of the disciple is to examine and discover the Dhamma for himself.

My teaching today and everyday, for you and for all people, is to live a life established in awareness and love so that you too may be free from your suffering."

The Buddha spoke always with words of kindness to promote love and harmony between all beings. However, he also instructed his followers to reflect and consider the teachings of Dhamma, and not just to follow blindly. This is not a religious instruction, it is a sharing of truth, and if we are always responsible for ourselves and our actions, we must be aware of what we do and how we live our life.

The blameless life is the highest life.

The first moral principle

As spiritual seekers, we undertake a personal rule of training, not to harm or kill another being, under any circumstances.

Not only will we refrain from harming or killing others, but we will actively care for and protect them - even if we don't like them - even if we are afraid of them. This is how we will train ourselves.

The second moral principle

As spiritual seekers, we undertake a personal rule of training, not to take anything that has not been freely given.
Not only will we refrain from taking from others, but we will actively be kind and generous towards them. This is how we will train ourselves.

The third moral principle

As spiritual seekers, we undertake a personal rule of training, not to take advantage of, or to use any position of authority over others, to manipulate them or the situation, to take what we want. Not only will we refrain from this, but we will actively support, protect and befriend others. This is how we will train ourselves.

The fourth moral principle

As spiritual seekers, we undertake a personal rule of training, not to use our speech in cruel and harmful ways. Not only will we refrain from this, but we will actively speak the truth kindly and gently. This is how we will train ourselves.

The fifth moral principle

As spiritual seekers, we undertake a personal rule of training, not to use any kinds of drugs to deliberately alter the consciousness.
Not only will we refrain from this, but we will actively

train ourselves to be aware and awaken from our delusion. This is how we will train ourselves.

As with every aspect of the spiritual path, these five moral principles are not to be followed blindly, or without investigation, and there should be no guilt involved if we are not able to live them to the very highest standard. But we do need to make the effort!
If we do not try, how will we change our life?

However, by continued practice of these principles, they will become naturally a part of who and what we are, and how we live. By reflecting on these principles they will become more and more refined, and rather than being intellectual or even academic issues, they will be natural and spontaneous manifestations of the compassionate heart. We will understand that this is the way that an enlightened being intuitively lives.

The Buddha lived in a time when animal sacrifice was common and seen to be an expedient way to appease the gods and request favours from them. The greater the sacrifice the bigger the favour, so on many, many occasions the streets of a town would run with the blood of helpless animal victims.
The Buddha also was seen by the brahmin priests of the time to be a socially dangerous man. He was eroding their power by proclaiming teachings of gender equality (on the spiritual path), and a life of harmlessness. Often whilst the Buddha was giving a discourse to the people, the brahmin priests would arrive to debate, and show their authority through Vedic knowledge and religious

power. On one of these occasions a group of priests arrived and in front of an audience spoke to the Buddha. "Venerable Gotama, you have a reputation as a great spiritual teacher, and so, with your permission, we would like to pose a question to you."

"Please ask anything you want," replied the Buddha.

"Master Gotama," continued the questioner, "We all know the value of sacrifice and how important it is, but can you tell us please, what is the true value of a cow, or ten cows or one hundred cows to be sacrificed? What is the true value of a sheep, or ten sheep, or one hundred sheep to be sacrificed? What is the true value of a horse, or ten horses or one hundred horses to be sacrificed?"

With the question finished the brahmins and the audience waited for the response.

Is it possible that the Buddha will show some anger or irritation to have such a question directed at him. What would he say? How could he respond when the question was phrased in such a way?

"My friend," began the Buddha, "You are correct. Sacrifice is a valuable practice and is truly important to our spiritual development, but if we have to sacrifice something, we must sacrifice our own greed and hatred and delusion, not the lives of helpless animals. It is easy for a man to take life, but harder for a man to live by honouring life. With greed, hatred and delusion gone from our lives we are able to live in the world free from fear, not only that, but free from inflicting fear onto others. Sacrificing one, ten or one hundred cows, sheep or horses will never bring a good result, but sacrificing our greed, or hatred or delusion, even for one moment, will bring only the best results for ourselves and for the world."

As always the Buddha shows his greatness through wisdom and love. He does not debate with, or attempt to humiliate the people who oppose him or his way. He can only share the truth. It is for others to accept or reject, as they choose. The truth for us all is the same, a life established in love and compassion is better for ourselves and better for the world.

Teaching to the Kalamas

…the Kalamas who were inhabitants of Kesaputta went to where the Blessed One was. On arriving there some paid homage to him and sat down on one side. Some exchanged greetings with him and after the ending of cordial memorable talk, sat down on one side; some saluted him raising their joined palms and sat down on one side, some announced their name and family and sat down on one side; some without speaking, sat down on one side.

The Kalamas who were inhabitants of Kesaputta sitting on one side said to the Blessed One, "There are some ascetics and brahmins, venerable sir, who visit Kesaputta. They expound and explain only their own doctrines, the doctrines of others they despise, revile, and pull to pieces. Some other ascetics and brahmins too, venerable sir, come to Kesaputta. They also expound and explain only their own doctrines, the doctrines of others they despise, revile, and pull to pieces. Venerable sir, there is doubt, there is uncertainty in us concerning them. Which of these reverend monks and brahmins spoke the truth and which falsehood?"

"It is proper for you, Kalamas, to doubt and to be uncertain. Uncertainty has arisen in you about what is doubtful. Come, Kalamas. Do not go upon what has been acquired by repeated hearing, nor upon tradition, nor upon rumour, nor upon what is in a scripture, nor upon surmise, nor upon an axiom, nor upon specious reasoning, nor upon a bias towards a notion that has been pondered over, nor upon another's seeming ability, nor upon the consideration, 'This one is our teacher.' Kalamas, when you yourselves know, 'These things are bad, these things are blameable, these things are censured by the wise, undertaken and observed, these things lead to harm and ill', abandon them.

What do you think, Kalamas? Does greed appear in a man for his benefit or harm?"

"For his harm, venerable sir".

"Kalamas, being given to greed, and being overwhelmed and vanquished mentally by greed, this man takes life, steals, commits adultery, and tells lies, he prompts another too, to do likewise. Will that bring about his harm and ill?"

"Yes, venerable sir."

"What do you think, Kalamas? Does hate appear in a man for his benefit or harm?"

"For his harm, venerable sir;"

"Kalamas, being given to hate, and being overwhelmed and vanquished mentally by hate, this man takes life, steals, commits adultery, and tells lies, he prompts another too, to do likewise. Will that bring about his harm and ill?"

"Yes, venerable sir."

"What do you think, Kalamas? Does delusion appear in a man for his benefit or harm?"

"For his harm, venerable sir."

"Kalamas, being given to delusion, and being overwhelmed and vanquished mentally by delusion, this man takes life, steals, commits adultery, and tells lies; he prompts another too, to do likewise. Will that being bring about his harm and ill?"

"Yes, venerable sir."

"What do you think, Kalamas? Are these things wholesome

or unwholesome?"
"Unwholesome, venerable sir."
"Blameable or not blameable?"
"Blameable, venerable sir."
"Censured or praised by the wise?"
"Censured, venerable sir."
"Undertaken and observed, do these things lead to harm and ill, or not? Or how do you understand it?"
"Undertaken and observed, these things lead to harm and ill. This is how we understand it, venerable sir."
"Therefore, did I say, Kalamas, what was said before, 'Come Kalamas. Do not go upon what has been acquired by repeated hearing, nor upon tradition, nor upon rumour, nor upon what is in a scripture, nor upon surmise, nor upon an axiom, nor upon specious reasoning, nor upon a bias towards a notion that has been pondered over, nor upon another's seeming ability, nor upon the consideration, 'This one is our teacher.'
Kalamas, when you yourselves know, 'These things are bad, these things are blameable, these things are censured by the wise, undertaken and observed, these things lead to harm and ill,' abandon them.'
Come, Kalamas. Do not go upon what has been acquired by repeated hearing, nor upon tradition, nor upon rumour, nor upon what is in a scripture, nor upon surmise, nor upon an axiom, nor upon specious reasoning, nor upon a bias towards a notion that has been pondered over, nor upon another's seeming ability, nor upon the consideration, 'This one is our teacher.' Kalamas, when you yourselves know, 'These things are good, these things are not blameable, these things are praised by the wise, undertaken and observed, these things lead to

benefit and happiness,' enter and abide in them.
What do you think, Kalamas? Does absence of greed appear in a man for his benefit or harm?"

"For his benefit, venerable sir."

"Kalamas, being not given to greed, and being not overwhelmed and not vanquished mentally by greed, this man does not take life, does not steal, does not commit adultery, and does not tell lies, he prompts another too, to do likewise. Will that bring about his benefit and happiness?"

"Yes, venerable sir."

"What do you think, Kalamas? Does absence of hate appear in a man for his benefit or harm?"

"For his benefit, venerable sir."

"Kalamas, being not given to hate, and being not overwhelmed and not vanquished mentally by hate, this man does not take life, does not steal, does not commit adultery, and does not tell lies, he prompts another too, to do likewise. Will that bring about his benefit and happiness?"

"Yes, venerable sir."

"What do you think, Kalamas? Does absence of delusion appear in a man for his benefit or harm?"

"For his benefit, venerable sir."

"Kalamas, being not given to delusion, and being not overwhelmed and not vanquished mentally by delusion, this man does not take life, does not steal, does not commit adultery, and does not tell lies, he prompts another too, to do likewise. Will that bring forth his benefit and happiness?"

"Yes, venerable sir."

"What do you think, Kalamas? Are these things wholesome

or unwholesome?"

"Wholesome, venerable sir."

"Blameable or not blameable?"

"Not blameable, venerable sir."

"Censured or praised by the wise?"

"Praised, venerable sir."

"Undertaken and observed, do these things lead to benefit and happiness, or not? How do you understand it?"

"Undertaken and observed, these things lead to benefit and happiness. This is how we understand it venerable sir."

"Therefore, did I say, Kalamas, what was said before, 'Come Kalamas. Do not go upon what has been acquired by repeated hearing, nor upon tradition, nor upon rumour, nor upon what is in a scripture, nor upon surmise, nor upon an axiom, nor upon specious reasoning, nor upon a bias towards a notion that has been pondered over, nor upon another's seeming ability, nor upon the consideration, 'This one is our teacher.' Kalamas, when you yourselves know, 'These things are un-wholesome, these things are blameable, these things are censured by the wise, undertaken and observed, these things lead to harm and ill,' abandon them.' Come, Kalamas. Do not go upon what has been acquired by repeated hearing, nor upon tradition, nor upon rumour, nor upon what is in a scripture, nor upon surmise, nor upon an axiom, nor upon specious reasoning, nor upon a bias towards a notion that has been pondered over, nor upon another's seeming ability, nor upon the consideration, 'This one is our teacher.' Kalamas, when you yourselves know, 'These things are good, these things are not blameable, these things are praised by the wise, undertaken and observed, these things lead to benefit and happiness,' enter and abide in them."

(excerpt from the Kalama Sutta)

The Other Shore

Part 2

Finding the Way

The Other Shore

The Four Noble Truths are the greatest truths.
The Eightfold Path is the greatest Path.
Freedom from desire is the best condition,
And he who has the eyes to see,
Is the best of men.

Dhammapada: Verse 273

The Other Shore

Finding the Way
(author's note)

I tell the story of the Buddha's training, enlightenment and subsequent teachings in my own words and according to my own understanding. I feel what I share to be true from my personal experiences of Dhamma, and the relationship I have developed with the Buddha and my own heart for more than thirty years of dedicated practice.

I do not believe that the Buddha ever spoke in lists. I feel that he shared Dhamma with those who sat in front of him and spoke in a natural, clear and loving way, not only using the common language of the people, but in terms that they could understand. His purpose in teaching was to share his own realisations, pointing the way to liberation for men and women, monks and nuns and the educated and uneducated equally.

He was not a religious leader, and so never had to defend or explain anything. His message was clear, 'Investigate for yourselves, so that you too will know the truth.' He told his disciples not to believe anything he said, but to test his words. These instructions have not changed in the two thousand six hundred years since the Buddha first shared the Dhamma in India.

I also do not ask anyone to believe or accept what I say, but only to follow the Buddha's teaching of Love and Awareness for themselves, and perhaps they will come to their own realisation as I have done, that is beyond religion, beyond books, beyond tradition.

The Other Shore

Finding the Way
Suffering, its cause, its cessation and the path

The enlightenment of the Buddha is said to have happened during a six hour period on the eve of his thirty fifth birthday preceding the full moon day of May. He sat in meditation under a large Pipal tree in the forest of Uruvela, close to the river Neranjara. Of course nothing can be sure, but for most of his life before those six hours he had been seeking enlightenment, or at the very least, questioning the life he led.
So powerful were these questions, that they had taken him away from a life of luxury, to a very different kind of life. The life of a wandering ascetic.

He was known now by his family name of Gotama, and had become famous for his extreme ascetic practices. So determined was he to find the answers to his questions, and so resolute was he in his endeavour, that he did not waste a single moment of practice. He followed the traditional ascetic path of self mortification, to punish and torture the body to free the spirit. He starved himself until he was living on only a tiny portion of rice and a handful of wild berries each day. He did not regard his health at all, and sat outside in meditation, without protection or shade, during the hottest part of the day. He meditated alone at night next to dead and decomposing human bodies, to test and push past his fear. He practiced holding his breath for long periods until (he said later in a conversation with Sariputta, his chief disciple) he could almost breath through his ears.
Although he had received some meditation instruction

from two well known teachers* at the beginning of his new life, neither could show him what he wanted to know.

Through their individual instructions he was able to attain very deep levels of concentration that would suspend the feelings of unsatisfactory-ness with life, but he could not maintain these states permanently.

At some point he would have to end his deep concentration sessions, simply to eat or bathe or go to the toilet. Although he excelled in these practices he was not satisfied. He told his teachers that he was looking for the permanent end to suffering, not just a temporary suspension of it. Even though they both asked him to stay and help teach this form of meditation to their groups, he declined. This was not the goal he was seeking. He left their company and, determined to find the complete ending to the unsatisfactory nature of his life, practiced alone.

Soon however, he was joined by five fellow ascetics who had trained with him earlier under his former teachers, and who were impressed by his incredible determination and endeavour. These ascetics now took him as their leader and together they trained for many years with Gotama always setting the example of intense determination.
One day Gotama was walking alone, far away from the others, when he suddenly fell. So many years of strict discipline and starvation had taken its toll.

Alarma the Kalama and Udaka Ramaputta

He lay in the dirt, too weak to raise himself up or even move, and waited to die. His desperation must have been enormous.

He reflected upon his early life and how he had always had everything he ever wanted, but he had renounced that for the holy life. A special endeavour for enlightenment, but even that noble intention had not been successful. He had lost everything for nothing, and now he waited to die, alone, lying in the dirt with the hot sun beating down on his back.

Fortunately a shepherd, grazing his sheep nearby, saw this almost dead skeleton figure in the dirt and stopped to help. He carried Gotama back to his small hut and began the process of nursing him back to health. Naturally it took many weeks to repair the damage done, and during this time Gotama, the great ascetic practitioner, again reflected on his life. He realised now that the body must be strong to continue this work, and that starvation and harsh treatment brought no good result. Now, and from the two essential qualities of love and compassion, he began to care for himself and eat again.

On one occasion during these weeks, Gotama was sitting outside the shepherds hut eating a bowl of milk rice, when the group of five ascetics saw of him. They were so shocked by this sight that they immediately broke all association with him. They felt betrayed by the one who was their leader and who had finally taken the easy road of sensual pleasure. They left the forest where they had all lived and trained together, and travelled to a small deer sanctuary, just outside Varanasi, to continue their practice alone.

Gotama, completely unaware of this, continued to make his body strong and healthy again so that he could continue with the work to be done. Now he remembered an incident from his childhood when he spontaneously entered a state of profound peace and calm and yet with a heightened sense of awareness. Without realising it he had stumbled into the practice of meditation (Vipassana) that would take him to enlightenment.

Now he knew what he must do.

Just to sit quietly and peacefully, to let go of any desire to get something special, but to see and know the mind.

At the moment when his desire, and his craving for a special state of illumination fell away, he was able to realise it. This was the condition for his enlightenment, the desireless state of being. To sit (in meditation) and not to want something. To meet the mind, the architect of his life, and to simply be with it, undisturbed by its contents, and without trying to hold on to something pleasant, or push away something unpleasant.

So he sat for six hours without intention, and as the full moon set, and the sun began to rise in the month of May at the beginning of his thirty fifth year, he opened his eyes, no longer as Gotama the Ascetic, but now as the Buddha, the fully awakened one. According to Theravada tradition, after the enlightenment, the Buddha stayed close to the same place in the forest for seven weeks, reflecting upon and comprehending what he had realised. The experience of enlightenment was not a verbal experience. It was not the realisation of a list of 'things'. It was a transcendent experience, beyond words, beyond description, beyond the rational, thinking mind. It was unconditional and unlimited freedom.

Immediately after the enlightenment, the Buddha decided that it would not be a good plan to teach this Dhamma. He felt that it would be difficult for him to share and that many people would only want to argue and harass him because it was outside their own levels of understanding. He felt that perhaps it would be better for him if he went somewhere quiet and spent his days alone, living a simple life and staying silent.

However, having spent some time in the forest, reflecting upon what had transpired, a great compassion arose in the Buddha and he knew that he must share what he had understood. Even though he felt that sometimes this would be difficult for him to do because of the minds of others, he must make this effort 'for the sake of those beings with only a little dust in their eyes'.

But how?

This experience was beyond language, how then could he use words to direct others along the path of liberation? What could he say?

At the end of seven weeks he knew what he must do, and so he set off from the forest of Uruvela towards Varanasi, the holy city of India, on the banks of the river Ganges.

This journey was by foot and so took many days. When he arrived in Varanasi he discovered that his five former colleagues, the ascetics who had trained with him for part of those important six years, were staying close to the great city, at a deer sanctuary called Isipatana. They were continuing with their ascetic practices and had no idea that Gotama was now enlightened. They also did not know the story of his recent near death experience from starvation, or his new understanding of the need for a strong and healthy body to walk this path.

The Buddha arrived at Sarnath, just outside Varanasi, and the deer sanctuary of Isipatana. He had come to offer something special, not to teach or proclaim, but to share his understanding and experience of liberation. He walked gracefully and unhurriedly towards his five former companions. When they saw him approaching in the distance they quickly had a small conference to decide how to act in front of this now perceived, 'weak practitioner'. They decided to ignore him. 'Let him come, let him be here, but don't speak or acknowledge him in any way'.

However, as the Buddha came closer, this hostility evaporated. The five ascetics could not help themselves. It was not possible for them to be angry or hostile towards this man. As he came even closer they found themselves moving towards him, offering him profound respect and friendship, taking his alms bowl, preparing a seat for him and washing his feet. He was different. They weren't quite sure how, but something profound, yet intangible had happened to Gotama. He was not the man they had left. Finally one of the ascetics asked the question the others wanted to ask.

"So, is it true, have you done it, have you realised the goal we have sought so long? Have you discovered the enlightenment?"

"Yes," he replied, "It is true, I have ended my journey, I have realised the enlightenment."

The group around Gotama were silent with these words. They knew that it could be true, but was it? He had always been the best of them, the most earnest, the most disciplined, the most resolute. He was the one who set the example and never rested from the hardest of their practices, and now everything he had worked for had been gained. Now they must know from him what he had understood.

"So, please, please share with us your understanding, so that we too might know for ourselves, that which you have realised."

And so the Buddha gathered around him his five former colleagues, and waiting for the perfect moment to speak, he began to share his understanding with others for the very first time.

The first teaching of the Buddha

So, if the experience of enlightenment is beyond words, what could the Buddha say? How could he transmit his understanding?
Traditionally he spoke about and explained the Four Noble Truths, (Cattari Ariya Sacca) but before this great teaching was collected, compiled and remembered as a list, how was it presented?

When we transmit the Dhamma to others, we speak from the heart and from our own direct experience. We are not trying to persuade, prove or show anything, but only to share our personal realisation of the truth.
In my own heart I feel that this must have been the case for Siddhartha. To speak lovingly and gently about that which truly cannot be expressed in words. To point the way with fingers of love.

"Friends," he began, "For six years I tried to find the key to enlightenment, and for this goal of perfect liberation I worked hard, and did not miss a moment to practice. I have meditated, starved myself and tortured and punished this body until it could bear no more. I collapsed in the dirt and I lay there waiting to die. Before my rescuer arrived to save my life, I realised that I had followed a wrong road, and that what faced me now was only the consequence of what I had empowered. These years of hard ascetic practices had not taken me nearer to enlightenment, only left me at the door of death. My kindly rescuer fed me with milk rice and slowly nursed me back to health. During those weeks I reflected on my life. I saw that my early days as a prince in the palace of my father, surrounded by luxury and wealth, had not helped me to understand the reason or cause of unhappiness, but at the same time, neither had my years of hard practice. I realised that these two extremes, one of indulgence in the world of the senses, and the other, the complete repression of the world of the senses, does not lead to liberation, only to more unhappiness in life, whether that unhappiness is experienced as gross or subtle. Friends, I have realised that there is a middle way - a transcendent way. Not a way between these extremes, but a way beyond them, and this way I have come to share with you."

First Noble Truth
Dukkha Ariya Sacca
The truth of suffering:

"My friends, when we look at our life, with eyes that are not clouded by views and opinions, by belief and superstition, and by delusion, what do we see? We see that it is exactly like this! Whether we like it or not, whether we approve of it or not, whether we agree with it or not, we see that life is exactly as it is.

As human beings we all face the same conditions of life, old age, sickness and death. We face separation and loss, suffering and unhappiness, in fact, we face everything that is possible for a human being to face, and why? Because we have life. That is all. There is no great god to punish you or reward you, to help you or persecute you, there is just life. But because of our delusion and non-understanding of reality, we personalise this life.

This life is not about us, we just make it about us, and so we experience the consequence of that, an endless feeling of unsatisfactory-ness.
Never having enough, always wanting more, and never, never being able to rest.
Life is just life, and everything else is delusion."

Second Noble Truth
Samodaya Ariya Sacca
The truth of the cause of suffering:

"So, if our life is 'just like this' what is the cause of our suffering? Why do we experience unhappiness when in reality the only thing we ever want is to be happy?

It is exactly because we do not accept this reality.

The cause of our unhappiness is not the world, or even the things and events in it, it is only this non-accepting mind. This mind filled with its desires and aversions, with its greed and hatred, with its fear.
It is because of this mind that arises and passes away endlessly, this mind that we call 'ours' but in reality cannot be owned or controlled, and that continually cries, 'it shouldn't be like this,' that we experience all the different manifestations of unsatisfactory-ness, what we call, unhappiness.
Unhappiness begins and ends in the mind. Each one of us is the architect of our life, experiencing the result of the desires, aversions and delusions we have empowered.
Only the mind is the cause of our unhappiness."

Third Noble Truth
Nirodha Ariya Sacca
The truth of the ending of suffering:

"But here now is the liberating truth.
If we are responsible for our unhappiness, and only us, then we are able to end that unhappiness. We don't have to wait for the world to be different for us to experience happiness, we just have to accept the reality of each moment. This can be done the instant we realise this truth. No-one causes the feelings we experience, they are just the past arising and our habit of acting on them. No-one can give or take away our happiness or our unhappiness. The conditions for the quality of our life lie directly within the mind. The moment we stop empowering the delusions that arise in the mind, we are free.
Truly this is the opportunity of human life, to free ourselves from the illusionary power of the mind."

Fourth Noble Truth
Magga Ariya Sacca
The truth of the way to end suffering:

"If we really want to be free, to live a life of love, peace and joy, we must make an effort, but that effort is intended not to get something, but to see something - to see and know this mind.
When we know the mind we are free.
So how can we know this mind?
Not by indulgence in it, and not by repression of it, but only by observing it clearly. Of knowing its movements, of knowing its fantasies, of knowing its fears, of knowing

its desires. When we know this mind we will understand the true nature of existence: that behind all phenomena there is only an emptiness, and by embracing and celebrating this emptiness we will end our suffering, and discover real and true happiness that we can then share with the world."

Eightfold Path
Magga
The Way:

"To realise the truth, and to experience the joy of liberation we must live a life that is beautiful, a life that is worthy. A life that has quality. We must empower love and wisdom in every moment, so that our life has value for ourselves and others.

We have to investigate and know beyond words, beyond belief and beyond culture, the reality of this being that we call self.

We must understand fully and truly, by our own investigation, the nature of this life until we are free from the delusions that fill the mind, and we must always make the effort, and support our intention to be free from these delusions.

We must speak in a way that brings harmony, love and wisdom to each situation, and we must live in the world in a way that does not bring harm to ourselves or others.

We must cultivate the effort and understanding, not to be lost in the fantasy of the mind, by developing a way of life supported by both an internal and external awareness, established upon a clear and focused mind.

If we can live from these principles, we can expect good

results."

The Buddha spoke in this way, not lecturing or trying to teach anything. Not trying to persuade or convince those who heard his words. He shared his simple message of love and wisdom for all to hear, and for all to follow - if they wanted to.

Nothing has changed since this first beautiful teaching was given to his five former associates at the deer park called Isipatana, two thousand six hundred years ago.

The truth waits for us all, if we truly have the mind and heart to practice.

The Middle Way

Traditionally, the teaching of the Buddha is known as the Middle Way, the way between extremes. However, this is not really accurate for it implies only a life of moderation - a little bit of this and a little bit of that. Not completely angry, only irritated, not completely happy, only pleased. Not completely wise, only intelligent.

The Middle Way of the Buddha is a gift to the world, for it shows the path to the complete realisation of the Truth and so the way to complete peace. This Middle Way is not a way between extremes, but the way beyond extremes. The transcendent way.

The understanding of this path is very important if we want to go beyond religion, and blind faith, personal views and opinions.

If we consider ourselves to be seekers of Truth.

The transcendent path that the Buddha revealed to his disciples at the Isipatana deer sanctuary, and then later to us, is the way to no longer be a prisoner of the mind, which is the sole cause of our suffering and unhappiness. Through the practice of a special form of meditation we can see the very nature of this mind, and by seeing, be free from its influence. By letting go of our attachment to the mind as being who and what we are, we can enjoy it when it presents something pleasant, and not suffer when it changes. But also, we can be with this mind peacefully when it presents something unpleasant, knowing intuitively, that it too will pass. Impermanence is the nature of all things. To harmonize and flow with this impermanence is to be one with the Truth itself, and is the nature of enlightenment.

This is the Middle Way. Not to get something, but to see something. To know directly the mind as the architect of our life, to wake up from our dream state of suffering, and to be free.

After hearing this most beautiful and profound first teaching, Kondañña, the eldest of the five former colleagues, and now disciples of the Buddha, understood completely and intuitively, that 'whatever begins must end'.

The Buddha saw this deep realisation in his eyes and exclaimed 'Kondañña knows, Kondañña knows'. From this moment of knowing, the disciple Kondañña was called Aññakondañña - Kondañña the Wise, and was the first person to realise enlightenment having been guided by the teaching of the Buddha.

Aññakondañña was the first Arahat* in the world.

*Arahat: A being enlightened through hearing and applying the teaching of a Buddha.

The Second Teaching of the Buddha

The day after the Buddha had explained the Four Noble Truths to his five, first disciples, he continued to share his understanding. To enlarge and make even clearer the conditions for our suffering and more importantly, how to be free from them, he gave his second great teaching. In modern terms we can explain this teaching as the Vipassana Koan*, a deep reflection into the nature of who and what we really are. The koan is presented like this:

> I'm not the body, I'm not the mind.
> What am I?

This is a deep and profound reflection and is the basis for the practice of continually dropping all our limiting ideas, established in attachment, to every aspect of mind and body.
If we are not the body, and if we are not the mind, who is it that suffers? Who is it that feels cold and pain? Who is it that lives? Who is it that dies?

Koan: From the Japanese Buddhist tradition of Rinzai Zen. It is a question, problem or story that defies the logical, thinking, rational mind. The koan is given to the disciple for his reflection and investigation until the mind is exhausted by thinking. At that time satori (profound insight) can arise.

The body is born, assumes its gender, takes its physical appearance, and journeys through its life. It meets old age, sickness and death, as an inseparable part of that journey. Even if we choose not to have these things, we cannot help but meet them. So here arises the profound question of Dhamma:

Is this body really ours? Does it do what we want it to do, or does it simply follow its own direction and its own dynamic through life? As with everything in Dhamma training and understanding, we have to go past a romantic view of our life, and come to the Truth.
The body exists and there is an connection with it, but is it ours, is it what we are?
The same reflection must be given to the mind and all its different aspects. The feelings, the perceptions, the thought processes and emotions (mental formations) and the sensory consciousness.
This mind is only an endless flow of these things, all continually arising and passing away. Where, in his process, can we find anything that is not already changing?

Are we ever able to determine our happiness in life simply through an act of will? Is it possible to decide to be happy in any moment and just that decision will suffice? When we engage in the real practice of meditation, not tied to technique or tradition, we will know from our own direct experience, the reality of this being that we call 'self'. We will know that behind all phenomena there is only an emptiness, no person, no abiding permanent persona.

The dropping of the delusion of 'self', of I, me, mine and my, is the liberation.

If there is no 'self', no identity that always has to be supported and maintained, defended and proclaimed, that is dependent on the ideas and views of others for its happiness, there can be no suffering, no guilt, no remorse, no lamentation.

Only the infinite joy of freedom. Of flowing peacefully, lovingly and harmoniously with life.

Only 'self' suffers, and in reality, 'self' is nothing more than a collection of ideas, views and opinions, arising and passing away in an endless stream, but behind those mental movements there is nothing substantial, just the continually changing and flowing mind.

When we pursue Truth with the attitude of the spiritual seeker, not concerned by dogma or belief, we will come to realise for ourselves, the very nature of the mind, and that in fact, the mind 'does not change, but that mind is change itself!'

The Third Teaching of the Buddha

A short time after the second teaching, and having travelled, talked to and inspired many people, the Buddha arrived again at the banks of the river Neranjara, close to the town of Gaya, and met three brothers named Kassapa. These brothers were all priests of the fire god Agni, traditionally one of the most important Vedic gods, and had between them many hundreds of followers.

The eldest brother, called Uruvela, was proud and arrogant and truly believed that he was enlightened, although the Buddha knew intuitively that this was not true.
However, the way of the Buddha is established in love and a non-conflicting relationship with others, and so he said nothing about this and only spoke pleasantly, quietly and with humility. He asked only if he might pass the night in the hall where the sacred fire was kept. Kassapa agreed that he could, but warned the Buddha that a powerful and enormous serpent (Naga) lived there, and that he would surely be killed. The Buddha thanked Kassapa for this consideration, but told him not to worry, he was sure that he would be safe.
The next morning of course, the Buddha appeared unscathed and Kassapa was impressed. He thought, 'this ascetic has great powers, but he is not enlightened like me!' However, there was also a kind nature to Kassapa and after this event he offered support to the Buddha, and provided him with alms food for many weeks.
During this time the Buddha stayed alone in a quiet grove close to the camp of Kassapa and his followers. Kassapa became more and more impressed after each

daily contact with the Buddha, and the way he naturally and spontaneously displayed himself, but still the thought that, 'this ascetic has great powers, but he is not enlightened like me!' stayed with him.

Now had come the time for the Buddha, acting only ever from great compassion for others, to speak the truth.

"Kassapa, my friend," began the Buddha, "I think that you are a kind and generous man, and only from my compassion for you and your followers, I feel that it is time for me to speak.

Kassapa, you are not enlightened, you are not an Arahat, and nothing that you do in your religious practice will take you to this place. The Dhamma is able to be understood by all, but beliefs and rituals only serve to obscure that understanding. Please allow me to help and share the Dhamma with you."

The heart of Kassapa opened, and he received and understood immediately the pure words of the Buddha. He truthfully admitted that what the Buddha had said was true, and humbly asked for a teaching for himself and his followers.

The Buddha agreed, and using analogies and symbols suitable for the recipients, gave the teaching that is known as 'The Fire Sermon'.

Again, here it is good to reflect upon the disposition of the Buddha.

He was not arrogant or conceited. He was not greedy for disciples or fame. He taught and shared his understanding, not to persuade or even demonstrate his superiority, but only for the benefit of others, so that their lives can be more beautiful from hearing the truth. When the Buddha spoke it was not to give a lesson or lecture, but only to share his love and wisdom.

The Teaching of Fire

"Friends, you all know the nature of fire. It burns, it consumes, but if you can look with eyes not clouded by superstition or belief you will see that in fact everything is burning, everything is on fire, and everything is being consumed.

The eye itself is on fire, and what it sees is on fire. The consciousness of the eye is on fire, and all the forms that the eye can see are on fire. The feelings that arise from seeing something are on fire, no matter if those feelings are pleasant, unpleasant or neutral.

And what is this fire that I speak about, this fire that burns and consumes everything?

It is the fire of greed, it is the fire of hatred, it is the fire of delusion. It is the fire of birth, it is the fire of aging, it is the fire of death. It is the fire of sorrow, it is the fire of regret, it is the fire of grief and it is the fire of despair.

When we look past the appearance of things we will see the truth, and from seeing that truth we will know the danger in living a life established in delusion and believing in the appearance of things.

It is the same for all the senses. The ear, the nose, the tongue, the body and the mind itself. These too are burning and being consumed. Whatever feelings arise from contacting the world through these senses are also on fire. Burning with the flames of greed, hatred and delusion. With the flames of birth, aging and death. With the flames of sorrow, regret, grief and despair.

When we know these truths directly, from our own

investigation, we experience a peaceful mind towards these things. By understanding and no longer seeking happiness through them, these fires die down and we are free. By not grasping or rejecting, and not being confused or overwhelmed by them we taste our own liberation. With this liberation we will know that we are truly free and that there is nothing more to be done for the fulfilment of our spiritual life."

The Four Noble Truths
(abridged version)

At one time when the Blessed One was staying at Isipatana Park, the deer sanctuary near Benares, he spoke to a group of bhikkhus*:

These two extremes, bhikkhus, should be avoided by one who has gone forth from the worldly life.
Sensual indulgence, which is low, coarse, vulgar, ignoble, unprofitable, and self-mortification, which is painful, ignoble and unprofitable.

Bhikkhus, the middle way, understood by the Tathagata, after he had avoided these two extremes, produces vision, produces knowledge and leads to calm, penetration, enlightenment and Nibbana.

Namely:
Right Understanding, Right Intention, Right Speech, Right Action, Right Livelihood, Right Effort, Right Mindfulness, Right Concentration.

This, bhikkhus, is the Noble Truth of Suffering:
Birth is suffering, decay is suffering, disease is suffering, death is suffering, association with unloved ones is suffering, separation from loved ones is suffering, not to get what one wants is suffering. In short, the five aggregates of grasping are suffering.

*Bhikkhu is the usual term now for a Buddhist monk.

This, bhikkhus is the Noble Truth of the Cause of Suffering:
The craving, which causes rebirth, is accompanied by passionate pleasure which takes delight in this or that object; namely, sensuous craving, craving for existence and craving for annihilation.

This, bhikkhus is the Noble Truth of the Cessation of Suffering:
The complete cessation, giving up, abandonment of that craving, release from that craving and the complete detachment from it.

This, bhikkhus is the Noble Truth of the Path leading to the Cessation of Suffering:
Right Understanding, Right Intention, Right Speech, Right Action, Right Livelihood, Right Effort, Right Mindfulness, Right Concentration.

(Dhammacakkappavattana Sutta)

Not body, Not mind
(abridged version)

"Bhikkhus, the body (material form) is not self. If the body was self, this body would not take us to suffering and we could say, 'let my body be like this', or 'let my body not be like this'.
But it is exactly because the body is not self, that it does take us to suffering, and that we cannot say 'let my body be like this', or, 'let my body be like that'.

"Bhikkhus, feeling is not self …"
"Bhikkhus, perception is not self …"
"Bhikkhus, mental formations are not self …"
"Bhikkhus, consciousness is not self …"

"Bhikkhu, how do you understand the body (material form), is it permanent or impermanent?"
"Impermanent, Lord."
"Is something impermanent pleasant or unpleasant?"
"Unpleasant, Lord."
"And is it good to consider that which is impermanent, unpleasant and subject to change as 'mine', 'what I am', and, my 'self'?"
"No, Lord."

"Bhikkhus, how do you understand the feelings …?"
"Bhikkhus, how do you understand perception …?"
"Bhikkhus, how do you understand mental formations …?"
"Bhikkhus, how do you understand consciousness …?"

"Therefore bhikkhus, any body (material form), whether past, future or present, internal or external, coarse or fine,

inferior or superior, far or near, should be understood as it really is with, understanding that, 'this is not mine, this is not what I am, this is not my self'".
"Any feeling whatever …"
"Any perception whatever …"
"Any mental formation whatever …"
"Any consciousness whatever …"
Seeing in this way, the wise disciple becomes dispassionate towards the body (material form), towards feelings, towards perceptions, towards mental formations and towards consciousness. By becoming dispassionate, lust fades away and his heart is liberated. When the heart is liberated there is the real understanding that future rebirths are finished, and what had to be done, has been done. Suffering has come to its end."

This is what the Blessed One said. The group of five bhikkhus were glad and they delighted in his words. Whilst the monks were listening to these words, their hearts were opened and they were liberated from their taints by freeing themselves of attachments. Now there were six Arahats in the world.

(Anattalakkhana Sutta)

The Fire Sermon

"Bhikkhus, everything is burning. What is the everything that is burning?

The eye is burning. Forms are burning. Consciousness at the eye is burning. Contact at the eye is burning. And whatever arises dependent on contact at the eye, experienced as pleasure, pain or neither pleasure nor pain, that too is burning. Burning with what? Burning with the fire of passion, the fire of aversion, the fire of delusion. Burning, I say, with birth, aging and death, with sorrows, lamentations, pains, distresses, and despairs.

The ear is burning. Sounds are burning. Consciousness at the ear is burning. Contact at the ear is burning. And whatever arises dependent on contact at the ear, experienced as pleasure, pain or neither pleasure nor pain, that too is burning. Burning with what? Burning with the fire of passion, the fire of aversion, the fire of delusion. Burning, I say, with birth, aging and death, with sorrows, lamentations, pains, distresses, and despairs.

The nose is burning. Aromas are burning. Consciousness at the nose is burning. Contact at the nose is burning. And whatever arises dependent on contact at the nose, experienced as pleasure, pain or neither pleasure nor pain, that too is aflame. Burning with what? Burning with the fire of passion, the fire of aversion, the fire of delusion. Burning, I say, with birth, aging and death, with sorrows, lamentations, pains, distresses, and despairs.

The tongue is burning. Flavours are burning. Consciousness at the tongue is burning. Contact at the tongue is burning. And whatever arises dependent on contact at the tongue, experienced as pleasure, pain or neither pleasure nor pain, that too is burning. Burning with what? Burning with the fire of passion, the fire of aversion, the fire of delusion. Burning, I say, with birth, aging and death, with sorrows, lamentations, pains, distresses, and despairs.

The body is burning. Touch sensations are burning. Consciousness at the body is burning. Contact at the body is burning. And whatever arises dependent on contact at the body, experienced as pleasure, pain or neither pleasure nor pain, that too is burning. Burning with what? Burning with the fire of passion, the fire of aversion, the fire of delusion. Burning, I say, with birth, aging and death, with sorrows, lamentations, pains, distresses, and despairs.

The intellect is burning. Ideas are burning. Consciousness at the intellect is burning. Contact at the intellect is burning. And whatever arises dependent on contact at the intellect, experienced as pleasure, pain or neither pleasure nor pain, that too is burning. Burning with what? Burning with the fire of passion, the fire of aversion, the fire of delusion. Burning, I say, with birth, aging and death, with sorrows, lamentations, pains, distresses, and despairs.

Seeing thus, the instructed noble disciple grows disenchanted with the eye, disenchanted with forms, disenchanted with consciousness at the eye, disenchanted with contact at the eye. And whatever arises dependent on contact at the eye, experienced as pleasure, pain or neither pleasure nor pain, with that too, he grows disenchanted.

He grows disenchanted with the ear, disenchanted with

sounds, disenchanted with consciousness at the ear, disenchanted with contact at the ear. And whatever arises dependent on contact at the ear, experienced as pleasure, pain or neither pleasure nor pain, with that too, he grows disenchanted.

He grows disenchanted with the nose, disenchanted with aromas, disenchanted with consciousness at the nose, disenchanted with contact at the nose. And whatever arises dependent on contact at the nose, experienced as pleasure, pain or neither pleasure nor pain, with that too, he grows disenchanted.

He grows disenchanted with the tongue, disenchanted with flavours, disenchanted with consciousness at the tongue, disenchanted with contact at the tongue. And whatever arises dependent on contact at the tongue, experienced as pleasure, pain or neither pleasure nor pain, with that, too, he grows disenchanted.

He grows disenchanted with the body, disenchanted with touch sensations, disenchanted with consciousness at the body, disenchanted with contact at the body. And whatever arises dependent on contact at the body, experienced as pleasure, pain or neither pleasure nor pain, with that too he grows disenchanted.

He grows disenchanted with the intellect, disenchanted with ideas, disenchanted with consciousness at the intellect, disenchanted with contact at the intellect. And whatever arises dependent on contact at the intellect, experienced as pleasure, pain or neither pleasure nor pain, he grows disenchanted with that too.

Disenchanted, he becomes dispassionate. Through dispassion, he is fully liberated. With full liberation, there is the knowledge of being, 'fully liberated.'

He discerns that 'destroyed is birth for me, the holy life has been fulfilled, the task is done. There is nothing further for this state of being.'"

That is what the Blessed One said. And whilst this discourse was being given, the hearts of the one thousand bhikkhus were liberated through no longer clinging to impurities.

(Adittpariyaya Sutta)

Part 3

Meditation, Acceptance and Love

The Other Shore

The one who meditates
On love and the Dhamma
Will realise Nibbana.

Dhammapada: Verse 368

The Other Shore

Meditation and Love
The foundations of the spiritual life

The teaching of the Buddha is deep, vast and profound, but its essential and enduring quality is its practicality in the lives of ordinary beings. Through his infinite compassion and love, the Buddha taught for forty five years, travelling throughout the northern parts of India. His message is as relevant today as it was all those years ago, because it is not cultural or gender oriented, it is only about our liberation from the conditions that lead to our unhappiness.

The Buddha taught a way to be free, not a way of blind faith or belief, and to walk this way we need only two things:

Awareness (Sati) to see things as they are, and Loving Kindness (Metta) to accept peacefully these things as they are.

The two qualities of Awareness and Love are like two hands that wash each other, both essential to the spiritual life, and both aiding and supporting each other.

Meditation
Bhavana

Awareness: *Sati*

If we truly want to see, know and comprehend reality, we must meditate. The meditation practice of Awareness is traditionally called Satipatthana, but in modern language we use the name Vipassana. This word does not describe a technique of meditation, but rather the purpose of that meditation - to see things as they really are.

There are many different schools, styles and forms of Vipassana practice, but in truth, anything that cultivates clear and unclouded vision of each moment can be called Vipassana. The Buddha himself did not prescribe a certain meditation technique for the development of awareness, rather he recommended that his followers (bhikkhus) be aware in every moment and in every action, both physical and mental. This practice of course, should be cultivated, not only in the formal sitting meditation, but in each moment of daily life.

Teaching of Awareness

"...Breathing in long, he is aware that he is breathing in long; or breathing out long, he is aware that he is breathing out long. Or breathing in short, he is aware that he is breathing in short; or breathing out short, he is aware that he is breathing out short. He trains himself to breathe in sensitive to the entire body and to breathe out sensitive to the entire body. He trains himself to breathe in calming bodily fabrication and to breathe out calming bodily fabrication. Just as a skilled turner or his apprentice, when making a long turn, discerns that he is making a long turn, or when making a short turn discerns that he is making a short turn; in the same way the bhikkhu, when breathing in long, discerns that he is breathing in long; or breathing out short, he discerns that he is breathing out short... He trains himself to breathe in calming bodily fabrication, and to breathe out calming bodily fabrication.

In this way he remains focused internally on the body in and of itself, or externally on the body in and of itself, or both internally and externally on the body in and of itself. Or he remains focused on the phenomenon of arising with regard to the body, on the phenomenon of passing away with regard to the body, or on the phenomenon of arising and passing away with regard to the body. Or his awareness that 'there is a body' is maintained to the extent of knowing and remembering. And he remains independent by not clinging to anything in the world. This is how a bhikkhu remains focused on the body in and of itself.
Furthermore, when walking, the bhikkhu is aware that he is walking. When standing, he is aware that he is standing.

When sitting, he is aware that he is sitting. When lying down, he is aware that he is lying down. Or whatever posture his body takes, that is how he is aware of it.

In this way he remains focused internally on the body in and of itself, or externally on the body in and of itself, or both internally and externally on the body in and of itself. Or he remains focused on the phenomenon of arising with regard to the body, on the phenomenon of passing away with regard to the body, or on the phenomenon of arising and passing away with regard to the body. Or his awareness that 'there is a body' is maintained to the extent of knowing and remembering. And he remains independent by not clinging to anything in the world. This is how a bhikkhu remains focused on the body in and of itself.

Furthermore, when going forward and returning, he makes himself fully aware. When looking toward and looking away he makes himself fully aware. When bending and extending his limbs he makes himself fully aware. When carrying his outer cloak, his upper robe and his bowl he makes himself fully aware. When eating, drinking, chewing, and tasting he makes himself fully aware. When urinating and defecating he makes himself fully aware. When walking, standing, sitting, falling asleep, waking up, talking, and remaining silent, he makes himself fully aware.

In this way he remains focused internally on the body in and of itself, or externally on the body in and of itself, or both internally and externally on the body in and of itself. Or he remains focused on the phenomenon of arising with regard to the body, on the phenomenon of passing away with regard to the body, or on the phenomenon of arising and passing away with regard to the body. Or his awareness that 'there is a body' is maintained to the extent of knowing and remembering. And he remains independent by not clinging to anything in the world. This is how a bhikkhu remains focused on the body in and of itself…"

The same applies to the feelings, the mind and the mental qualities.

(excerpt from Mahasatipatthana Sutta)

Love
Metta

Love is a word in our language that we use often, and so it is easy for us to misunderstand the real significance of it when we refer to 'Spiritual Love'.
In usual speech, to love someone or something is to establish a relationship to it based in an attachment. However, it is that very attachment that creates the condition for our suffering or unhappiness in the future.

At one time the Buddha was sitting with King Bimbisara. The king, who was already a lay disciple and prominent supporter of the Buddha, asked a question.
"Master, in the world there seems to be so much suffering and pain, but I would like to know where suffering and pain really begins?"
"Your majesty, all suffering and all pain begins with love and attachment."
The king could not accept this answer, and so, in front of the Buddha and without reflection, he rejected this reply.
"No, no, no, this cannot be true, there must be something else, something you are not telling me. I ask you again, please tell me truly, where does suffering and pain really begin?"
"Your majesty," answered the Buddha, "I tell you truly that all suffering and all pain begins in love and attachment."
For the second time this answer was rejected and the question was asked again. The Buddha, speaking only from truth and wisdom, replied for the third time in the same way.

At this point the king relaxed, and letting go of his resistance to the truth, and his fixed views of life asked the Buddha to explain his answer.

"Your majesty," began the Buddha, "Imagine that your son was kidnapped by bandits and held to ransom. These bandits threatened to torture horribly your son, and eventually kill him if the ransom was not met. Now, I ask you to tell me, how you think you would feel?"

"This would be something terrible for me," said the king, "A tremendous suffering in my life and a tremendous pain in my heart. I cannot imagine anything more horrible. Naturally I would comply completely with the demands of the bandits and do anything for the safe and speedy return of my son."

"Now, your majesty," continued the Buddha, "Imagine the same situation with someone else, not your son but the son of a neighbouring king. In this instance, how do you think you would feel?"

"Well," began the king, "the situation is still horrible of course, but naturally for me it would not be the same, and I would not suffer or feel pain in my heart as I would for my own son."

"So you see your majesty;" concluded the Buddha, "The cause behind all of the suffering and pain that we meet in our life, is only our love and attachment for people and things. Without this attachment there can be no suffering."

Whatever we are attached to will hurt us.

Perhaps, without real reflection and understanding, this short story will imply that we should not love anyone or become close to anything. This of course is not the case.

All romantic and emotional love is an attachment to another. Because of this attachment we will experience suffering, large or small, gross or subtle, immediately or sometime in the future. It is a simple equation and needs only a little, but honest reflection of our own life. Suffering, unhappiness, stress, jealousy, uneasiness, fear is the consequence of an attachment. If we have no attachment, we have no grounds for our suffering.

We love our children because they are our children. We love our football team because it is our football team. We love our partner because they are our partner. If our children are injured or fail in something, we suffer. If our football team plays badly and looses, we suffer. If our partner is ill, or cannot live up to our expectations of how they should be, we suffer.

Our attachments are endless and include also material objects and even the contents of our mind, our ideas, our views and our opinions. More subtly, and without realising it, we are attached to our own suffering and unhappiness, even if we believe that we are not.

Suffering is conditioned by attachment, and the antidote to that suffering is Spiritual Love.

> The wise ones walk easily
> Attached to nothing.
> They are neither elated by happiness
> Or downcast by sorrow.

Dhammapada: Verse 83

Loving Kindness
Metta Bhavana

In spiritual terms, Love means to be completely open and accepting of the conditions and events of the moment, whatever those conditions and events are. Having accepted without reservation we can respond. And because we have accepted without limitations, the reality of the moment, we can respond with Love, rather than with fear.

It's simple, but not easy.

If our child is ill we must accept because whether we want it or not, it is the reality of the moment. It is beyond our liking or disliking, it is the truth of the moment. Once we have accepted this truth we can respond. We can do whatever is necessary.

The development of Love in our life is a truly important practice, for real power and beauty lies only in the loving heart. With love as our basis for thought, speech and action, we can never be manipulated or controlled by others, or fall into the trap of judging, criticising and even condemning them simply because they are not the way we think they should be.

As the fear that we carry within us, and that determines the quality of our life disappears, the loving heart opens and we taste the joy of living fully here and now. No longer conditioned by the past or in anticipation of the future.

The Buddha's teaching for a life of love is not just a fanciful idea, inspiring to dream about, but not really possible to apply. As with everything he taught, it is practical and relevant to our modern everyday life, and is established in two things: the intuitive and non judgemental realisation that as long as beings are unenlightened they will live from the perspective of greed, hatred and delusion, and so are capable of any kind of horrible and un-just action; and that a life established in love is possible for everyone.

Attachment
Upadana

At one time the Buddha was living together with a number of disciples in a glade, close to a forest. The life here was quiet and simple, collecting alms food in the morning from the nearby village, and passing the rest of the day listening to the teachings of the Buddha, and engaged in meditation practice.

One day a small group of Bhikkhus approached the Buddha and asked his permission to go further into the forest and continue their meditation there.

The Buddha gave his consent, but reminded the bhikkhus that the practice of awareness is not about a physical posture, a time or a special place, it is only about being aware of this body and this mind in every moment as they continually change and flow.

The bhikkhus acknowledged this advice from their teacher, but were determined to follow their original idea, and so they respectfully bowed and left. Having walked a short way into the forest they came to a huge tree standing in a clearing. This tree, they thought, would be perfect for them, as they could stay as a group sitting around the base and meditating together.

This they did, and everything began well.

However, this tree was the home to many forest spirits and ghosts, and although at the beginning they were happy to accommodate disciples of the Buddha, as the time passed they grew impatient for the bhikkhus to leave.

"How much longer will they stay?" they asked each other, "This is our home and we want it back. These bhikkhus have to leave!"

But how to make the meditators break their concentration and depart? This was the question that the spirits and ghosts reflected upon, until finally they arrived at the answer. They were spirits and ghosts after all, and the bhikkhus, even though they were disciples of the Buddha, were in reality still only men. It seemed that it would not be too difficult to appear in front of them, in the guise of spectres and evil demons, and frighten them so much that they would leave.

Silently the bhikkhus continued with their meditation until the moment when the tree dwelling spirits put their plan into action! Out of the forest came a hoard of screaming ghosts and demons, circling the bhikkhus and calling for them to leave. The plan worked and the bhikkhus were terrified. They immediately stood up, and as a group, raising their robes above their knees, ran as fast as they could back to the Buddha.

Back at the camp of the Buddha, red faced and gasping for breath, they sought an audience with their great teacher to tell him what had happened. The Buddha received them and listened patiently to their story. The bhikkhus then asked how they could overcome or destroy these demons? The Buddha waited until they were calm and composed again and ready to receive the teaching, and then spoke.

"My friends, only fear has power in our life. The moment we empower our fear and are afraid, we become helpless victims to the circumstances. Who knows the extent of what we can do or say?

Friends reflect, only when fear is present in our life at any moment can we be manipulated or coerced by others. Fear is the enemy to peace and to love in our life, and is that which needs to be transcended in the spiritual life. Our practice then, is not to overcome or destroy these spirits of the forest, or any other living beings, but to live peacefully with them, accepting them for who and what they are, and not demanding that they be different, so that we can feel secure.

You must understand that beings are the way they are, and that is their choice, but you are the way you are, and that is your choice. So now, my friends, as disciples of Dhamma, how do you choose to be?

If you choose the path of love and compassion, you will be free from fear and experience a life of joy and celebration. If you choose a life of fear, you will stay in the clutches of the world. No matter how clever or intelligent you are, with fear as the basic condition for your life, you will always be a victim to it, and so always suffer. So, my dear friends of Dhamma, what do you choose?"

Inspired by the beautiful words of the Buddha the bhikkhus answered in unison, "Master, we choose a life of love."

"Very well," continued the Buddha, "Here is a practice for you all, so that you may be happy and free from fear in your life, and then share that happiness with all beings. Return to the forest and the tree you have meditated under. As you leave me now and as you proceed on your journey let your minds be filled only with love, acceptance and compassion for these spirits of the forest, and all other beings. Let your thoughts of loving kindness radiate outward from fearless heart to include everything that has life, whether we can see it or not, or whether we can touch it or not. From this moment now live from the compassionate feeling that wishes only happiness and safety for others, so that everything that exists may be well and live in peace."

The bhikkhus were inspired and revitalised by these words, and immediately returned to the forest, this time following the teaching of the Buddha.

When the spirits and ghosts saw them returning they were immediately angry, and resolved to this time, do harm to the invaders of their forest, but this anger dissolved quickly as the bhikkhus came closer expressing only compassion and the state of non-conflict towards all beings. Experiencing the power of love directed towards them the spirits immediately made available their home for the bhikkhus to use for their meditation, and were happy to do so.

Without fear there can be no fighting, no war, no persecution and no violence in the world, but who is it that will change this situation?

It seems that we always wait for the other to change before we ourselves will act from goodness, or purity, but the way of love is not like this.

The fighting will stop when we stop fighting. It is this simple.

Before we can argue for world peace and a beautiful social order, we have to learn how to live with our own families and friends, our work colleagues and society members. The power of Love is overwhelming, and when we are free from fear, we project this beautiful power into our own life and our immediate environment. Do not think that a small, but good action has no value in the world, or that a small harmful action goes unnoticed by the universe.

> Let no-one think of wrong doing,
> 'The consequence will not touch me'.
> Little by little the pot is filled,
> And little by little the foolish one
> Becomes filled with wrongdoing.

> Dhammapada: Verse 121

> Let no-one think of good action,
> 'The consequence will not touch me'.
> Little by little the pot is filled,
> And little by little the wise one
> Becomes filled with beauty.

> Dhammapada: Verse 122

Teaching of Loving Kindness

This is what should be done by those who are able to be pure, and who wish to know the path of peace.

They should be able, upright, perfectly upright, gentle, obedient and humble. Contented, easily supportable, with few duties and responsibilities, of right livelihood, with senses calmed, discreet, not impudent and not greedily attached to family. They should not do even the smallest thing for that wise people would later blame them for. They should always be thinking, may all beings be happy and secure, may their hearts be wholesome.

Whatever living beings there may be, feeble or strong, tall, stout or medium, long, short or small. Seen or unseen, those dwelling far or near. Those who are born and those who are to be born, may all beings, without exception, be happy.

Let none deceive another, or despise any being in any place. Let none through anger or ill will wish harm upon another. Just as a mother protects her only child at the risk of her own life, so too should one cultivate a boundless heart towards all beings. Let their thoughts of Love pervade the whole world, above, below and across, without any obstruction, without any hatred, without any fear. Whether they are sitting, standing, walking or lying down, as long as they are awake they should cultivate this reflection. This they say, is the highest teaching.

By not holding on to fixed views, the pure hearted ones, being free from sense desires and having clarity of vision, are not born into this world again.

(Metta Sutta)

The Other Shore

Part 4

Crossing the River

The Other Shore

You yourselves must make the effort,
Buddhas only point the way.
Those who have entered the Path
And who meditate
Will be freed from the ties of delusion.

Dhammapada: Verse 276

The Other Shore

Crossing the river
The work that needs to be done,
has to be done by ourselves.

Dhamma is the simple, but profound truth to be experienced by everyone. If we make the effort we will receive the result of that effort. If we make no effort, we will receive the result of making no effort. If you really want to test your Dhamma understanding, look at your life. Here, if you are brave and honest, you will see everything.

The spiritual life is not only a life of meditation. It is a life of living, of being in the world with our friends and our family. Of working and sharing the beauty of our heart. Therefore our practice must exist in this place also. If we are sincere in our intention to be free, we will use every opportunity to open and pass through the doors that make our prison. This journey can feel at times to be long and difficult, but we have to make the effort - we have to! The other shore is directly in front of us, just waiting for our arrival. Be strong, be determined, be clear.

Here then, are ten simple but important exercises to bring the joy and beauty of Dhamma into your daily life.

The real question for you now is,

> 'Do I really want to practice or not?'

The Other Shore

Focus

Give your full attention to whatever you are doing, no matter how trivial it may seem. Not in a special meditative way, but just naturally, being in the moment for the moment.

It is a common misconception that we are able to perform many different activities at the same time. In truth we only end up doing all badly. So take care, and give yourself fully to the task in hand.

We often complain about interruptions, and about not being able to 'get on' with our work, and so because of this attitude we suffer irritation, annoyance and frustration. In fact, all that has really happened is that we have, in that moment, stopped flowing with the ever changing conditions of life.

When we can learn to accept work, and the whole of our life, as a series of events continually beginning and ending, we can easily be with each one as it arises. We can flow with life itself.

If, for example, we are writing a letter with the feeling of impatience, wanting to finish what we are doing without interruption, and the telephone rings, we may slam down our pen, pick up the telephone with a sigh and speak abruptly to the person on the other end. If it turns out to be a wrong number, everything suddenly seems a hundred times worse, and we return to our letter tutting and shaking our head. With this kind of attitude nobody benefits. You feel irritated because you cannot 'get on', and the person who called you is upset at your brusque and off hand attitude.

However, if we can follow the flow of events without

resistance, then our attitude to the moment is one of love, and not anger, and this is expressed in the way we respond.

Even though we are occupied with our important activity, when the telephone rings we will be able to stop writing the letter completely, and turn our full attention to the call. Because we are not carrying an idea of how this moment should be, we will speak kindly and politely to this person who has just entered our life, and naturally be as helpful as possible. When our conversation has ended we will turn our attention away from the telephone call, and return completely, to writing our letter.

This way everyone benefits. You benefit because you are not lost in anger and irritation, and the other person benefits because they met only kindness and respect.

Every day at home or at work, we must open doors, and this simple action can be a wonderful way to focus.

The moment your hand touches the door handle, pause and bring your attention to it. How does it feel? Just notice, no need to make a scientific analyses, just be aware. Notice the temperature. Notice the texture. Notice what can be noticed. This moment of awareness is enough to bring your whole life back into focus, back into balance. Now, before you open the door, resolve to leave any unpleasant mind states you are experiencing in the room that you are leaving. Don't take them with you, but enter the next room soft and new. Gently exhale, feel the body relaxed, and smile. Who knows what wonderful thing awaits you.

With awareness, and the intention to practice, everything

can be used to re-focus and re-centre us in our life. When we are able to cultivate the habit of focus in all our activities, nothing will be seen as an interruption or disturbance, and we will be truly flowing with life.

Stay soft

The body is the mirror of the mind. Here there can be no secrets because nothing can be hidden. The mind is revealing itself in the body at all times, and in all things. So, if you truly want to know the real condition of the mind, look to the body. How does it feel - just in this moment? Do you feel any tension or uneasiness? Relax and allow your body to reveal your true mind state.

If there is tension, don't try to change it or push it away, just relax, let it be there. Now, close your eyes and gently exhale. Let your shoulders drop. The shoulders are a good stress indicator. If they are high and tight it is a clear signal that you are not centred. Let them relax and fall back into their natural position. Remember that stress has no beneficial qualities in your life, and a life without stress is a life with real value. A life where we can serve ourselves and the other.

Take a few relaxing breaths, allowing the exhalation to be gentle but as long as possible without straining, even letting the breath stop for a moment when it is finished before inhaling again. On the inhalation, let your awareness rest at the nostrils and simply feel the breath returning into the body.

Another simple technique to create the environment where the body can return to a natural and relaxed condition is called 'The Golden Halo'.

The Golden Halo.

Find a quiet place away from other people and where you will not be disturbed. Stand in a relaxed posture with your arms hanging naturally by your side, and your feet approximately shoulder width apart. Lightly close your eyes and imagine a large golden halo above your head. The quality of this halo is to be beautiful and loving. Now, slowly allow this halo to pass down over your body feeling each part it passes over becoming soft and relaxed. When it reaches the soles of your feet, you are finished. This relaxing and centring practice will take only one minute to complete, and you will return to your previous activity renewed and refreshed.

The body cannot lie, so the moment you notice any tension at all, create the mental environment to let it go.

Listening

When listening to other people, really listen. Don't anticipate what you think they are going to say.

We send messages to each other, not only through our words, but rather through subtle nuances and gestures. When we are interested in the other person we will listen with our whole body, and perhaps see or feel what is behind the words used.

Our usual way of communicating is not to listen at all, but to wait (if we are able) until the other person has paused so that we can say what we want to say, often completely unconnected with the real theme of the dialogue.

If we listen 'purely', without anticipation or judgement we may find that we are understanding something that we had previously been blind to.

In this way we serve the other by making the space for them to show themselves.

When we can see the 'real person' with their fears and difficulties in life, behind what they think they show through their words, we are better able to be of help, and contribute something worthy and of value to each and all our relationships.

Speaking

Speech is our main form of communication, but as an ability only human beings can perform it is not always used to its fullest potential. Just reflect, what do you talk about? The weather? Television programmes? Food? Holidays? Other people? Yourself?

When we walk on this Dhamma path we need to consider; How important is what I want to say? Will I benefit from saying it? Will the other person benefit from hearing it? These are important questions for the disciple, and very often the best way to use our speech is to remain silent and not to continually give our views and opinions as to how everyone and everything should be. When we really understand the power of speech, we will want to use it as a tool to heal and unite people, not cause further division in the world.

This does not mean that we should never be frivolous or engage in casual conversation, but we should make the effort to be aware of what we say, and the value of it. Our speech should be honest and kind, and even if we need to assert ourselves, we can do it gently with words that are not offensive or insulting. In fact a quite and polite but determined refusal to accept an unacceptable situation is much more powerful than resorting to abuse and insults. Speech is a tremendous power in every situation because it can be used to cut or inspire.

With our words we can promote love or fear, tolerance or hatred, compassion or cruelty.

When our speech is used wisely we stay centred and enjoy the results of balance in our life.

Shouting

The simple rule is DON'T.
Shouting across a room or up the stairs is a lazy and disrespectful way of communicating with others. If you have something to say to a person, go to them, speak to their face and give them your full attention. Make that moment of communication the most important thing at that time. It is a fact that people respond to how we treat them, and if we show respect it will be returned, although due to habits gathered in the past it may take some time. Shouting of course is often a manifestation of anger, however, even if it feels good in the moment, it is always counter productive. Reflect, how do you feel when you are being shouted at? Why should anyone else feel differently?

Speech as we have already seen, is a powerful tool at our disposal, and with it we can build bridges to love, or continue the divisions in life through fear. Look at our political and religious leaders when they address their followers. What do they say, and how do they say it? With love or aggression? If we take our examples in life to be men and women engaged on a real spiritual journey we will want to emulate their style. People like the Buddha and the Zen Masters. People like Gandhi and the Dalai Lama. Listen to their words and how they speak.

Love is never shouted, it is a gift gently offered to the world.

Resentment

In order to live peacefully and harmoniously and bring benefit into our life and into the lives of others, we need to leave the past where it belongs. In the past!
Whenever we carry slights, hurts, insults and grudges, it is only ourselves that suffer. We remember an incident from perhaps twenty years ago or only yesterday, and in that memory all the unpleasant feelings arise and we re-live the experience and so suffer. Not the person you are thinking about, not the one who hurt you, just you. The other person may have completely forgotten the incident, or not even been aware that they had upset you. But you carry it, and you remember it, and you suffer as a consequence.
We need to start each day, and each moment anew. Carrying the past blocks our potential for the future, and in this situation we are always the victim. Victim of our own mind!

At one time there were two Buddhist monks walking along a country road after a heavy rain. As they rounded a bend they saw that the road was flooded and standing on this side of the water was a young and beautiful woman. It was obvious that she wanted to cross the water, but obvious too that she did not want to get her clothes dirty and wet. Without hesitation one of the monks swept the young woman up in his arm and carried her through the water. The other monk followed behind in silence. Reaching the far side of the water the monk put the young woman down, and having been joined by his companion continued on his way to the monastery

where they would spend the night. At the gates of the monastery the second monk, no longer able to stay quiet, spoke:
"Excuse me," he said, "But I must speak! We monks are not supposed to even look at young and beautiful women, and certainly not pick them up and carry them. Why did you do that?"
The other monk answered, "I left that woman standing by the side of the water, do you still carry her?"

The practice of Loving Kindness is invaluable for helping to release us from the past. One simple formula for this beautiful practice is this:
Sit quietly for a few moments, allowing the body to soften and relax, gently keeping the attention with the natural flow of breath, and repeat mentally three or four times:

May I accept others exactly as they are in this moment.
May I accept this moment exactly as it is.
May I accept myself exactly as I am in this moment.

This simple yet powerful practice allows all our judgements of ourselves and others to fall away, so that we can be at peace with everyone and everything, even if we don't like them or approve of what they do. It may seem that Loving Kindness will make us weak in front of others, even to the point of being a victim to their perceived personal power, but in fact the opposite is true. From the position of being non-judgemental we become stronger and more confident, able to assert ourselves if necessary, though not through anger or fear, but through patience, kindness and acceptance, the manifestations of Love.

'Beings are the way they are - that is their choice.
You are the way you are - that is your choice.'

So, how do you want to be?
A prisoner of your past, or free to live fully and completely in each moment? Learn to cultivate love and acceptance in your life so that you can be free from your past. The past has gone, all that is left is a memory, and a memory is only a movement of mind. Accept others as they are and you will be stronger, gentler and more independent. You will be better able to fulfil your real potential as a human being, and be a blessing to all those around you.
A more traditional form of loving kindness meditation is below. The rule is always the same, 'to change our life we must make the effort,' and if we apply earnestly the practice of love to our life, we will see everything open in front of us, like a flower in springtime.
Sit quietly each day and make this recitation, empowering each word so that it becomes who you are - a being that lives beautifully from a fearless and loving heart.

May I be free from anger and ill will.
May I be free from fear and anxiety.
May I be free from suffering and pain.
May I be free from ignorance and desire.
May I be happy and peaceful.
May I be harmonious.
May I be liberated from greed, hatred and delusion.
May I realise the deeper peace within.
May all beings be free from anger and ill will.
May all beings be free from fear and anxiety.
May all beings be free from suffering and pain.

May all beings be free from ignorance and desire.
May all beings be happy and peaceful.
May all beings be harmonious.
May all beings be liberated from greed, hatred and delusion.
May all beings realise the deeper peace within.

Awareness

Give awareness to what you do, enjoy it if possible, but be aware. Our usual way of living is to be unaware. We don't really see what we do and so understand and accept the consequence of it. However, this can change if we give attention to our actions.

Awareness is the most powerful force in changing our life from stressful to peaceful, and from unhappy to happy. To know, without judgement or even comment, exactly who and what we are and to live in the world from that basis.

Unawareness is like being asleep. Notice any busy street. People walking one way whilst looking another. How can we see what is in front of us when we are looking somewhere else? How can we find the truth when we look in the wrong place? It is no wonder that when we live like this we can often feel to be victims of life. Of course, there is no universal plot against you, you're just asleep in your life - wake up! It's time to wake up!

Witnessing.

A simple awareness practice to take into your daily life is called witnessing, of being the observer of your actions.

Simply telling yourself what is happening and what you are doing.

For example: I am walking down the street. I am drinking my coffee. I am washing my hands, etc.

We can also witness our feelings and emotions, but as always, without judgement.

For example: I am feeling tired. I am feeling happy. I am feeling irritated. I am feeling angry.

To witness in this way helps us not to be lost in the situation, and so be better able to respond in a loving, gentle and wise way. Without 'self' awareness we tend to react blindly, being swept away by our emotions and our old mental habits. With awareness we will recognise the different states of mind that continually arise and pass away, and respond accordingly. Reaction comes from being asleep, from being lost in the fantasy of the mind. Response comes from being awake, of seeing the reality and no longer being deluded by the appearance of things.

Quality time

This is something that, like so many things on the spiritual path, is not clearly understood.

Give yourself quality time. Don't try to find it, but make it! Prioritise it!

Happiness is something that we share with the world, but happiness is hard to find when we are tired and living under conditions of stress, so take care of yourself! Make the time for your happiness.

Set aside parts of the day just for you. Take the telephone off the hook when you eat your meal or take your bath or shower. If you miss a phone call, what do you really miss?

Be still, sit quietly and relax. Read a book or watch your favourite DVD or video. Enjoy the moment of pleasure. Pamper yourself.

We have the same right to happiness as everyone else, not more, but not less either - and this includes our children and partners. Perhaps you think that this attitude is selfish (social conditioning, not reality), but reflect, when you are tired, upset or angry, how much happiness will you bring into the lives of others?

We share our feelings with everyone we come into contact with. When we are depressed we share that, when we are angry we share that. Whatever we feel we share, even if we make an effort to hide it. The mental state experienced at that moment will always make itself known through a gesture or a word and be passed on to the other.

When we are happy, relaxed and at ease, because we have spent quality time on ourselves, we share that also.

We become a joy to be with and so everyone benefits for our care and attention to ourselves.

We need to understand that we are all important, and that we all have the right to the best. So treat yourself. Give yourself the same love and attention you would give your children or partner or parents, and be happy. You deserve it.

Smile

A smile is the expression of our heart. It comes from happiness. We don't smile when we are stressed or unhappy, but by 'witnessing' and relaxing we can change that.

The next time you feel stressed, try to witness the feelings you experience, don't judge, just notice. Soften the body and let the smile come through. The realisation of Dhamma is that everything we experience only has the power that we give it, so don't give unpleasant feeling any power, just let them go, and feel the joy of that, of no longer being a victim to the mind.

A smile is the manifestation of happiness, and happiness is our natural state of being. We don't have to create it, we just have to let go of the things that obscure it.

The equations in Dhamma practice are always very simple.

> If we let go a little, there is a little happiness,
> If we let go a lot, there is a lot of happiness,
> If we let go completely, complete happiness.

We spend a lot of time trying to be happy, attempting to organise everyone and everything to be just the way we want them to be, but this is an endless task, and takes us only to disappointment and more unhappiness.

However, it is possible to accept people and situations as they are, without judgement or condemnation, and so be happy. This does not mean that we will be victims to others, only that we accept the situation truly as it is and then respond. Then we have it!

When we stop trying to create happiness, it comes by itself.
So relax, smile and be happy.

Meditation

There are many different types and styles of meditation, from simple relaxation techniques, to the most profound practices of Satipatthana (Vipassana), but whatever the style, they all require the same thing from you. Effort!
If you really want to change your life you yourself must make the effort, no-one can do it for you.

It is true that meditation established in the practice of awareness (Sati) and love (Metta) is the key to changing our life, because it is only through awareness and love that we can transcend the illusion of 'self', and therefore the unhappiness that this illusion brings. When we have awareness we are able to see and know the reality of this being that we call 'self'. When we have love, we are able to accept this being without conditions.
Awareness is not a belief or blind faith, it is the direct and personal investigation into the real cause of our unhappiness in life, manifesting as stress, anger, fear, frustration and all the rest. When we understand, from our own direct experience, exactly where these things begin, we are in a position to finally do something about them, namely, let them go, let them all go!
All our unhappiness and suffering comes from ourselves. It is always the reaction to a situation that causes our suffering, never the situation itself. The situation is just the situation. Our reaction or response will dictate our experience of happiness or unhappiness. Simply put, the world we experience is the one that we create for ourselves, moment after moment. This world is unique and personal to us.

No-one has the power to make you angry. Anger arises within us. It is the same with all our mind states. If we identify with them, we become them and so suffer. With the cultivation of Loving Awareness we can experience anger, and not be angry. Fear, and not be afraid. Depression and not be depressed.

Loving Awareness is the path we each have to walk. To see the mind and not be afraid. To know the mind and not to judge ourselves for its content. To let go of our continual and habitual identification with this mind as being who, and what we are.

The mind is not what we are, it is only that which we become.

When we stop 'becoming' these endless and ever changing mental states we will be free, and our lives will express that freedom. A life where we are no longer the victim, but the master. A life of love, joy and peace. A life that is a blessing to ourselves and all the beings we share our planet with.

Simple Awareness Meditation.

Sit comfortably in a chair and let the eyes close naturally. Awareness is a condition of the mind, not of physical posture, so it is not necessary to sit 'Buddha' style on the floor, unless you are able to do so comfortably. Keep the back straight without tension, let your hands rest in your lap and place your feet flat on the floor. Do not allow the head to fall forward. Imagine someone will take your photograph whilst you are meditating, so maintain the best and most elegant posture you can.

Without trying to control the breathing in any way, take your awareness to the breath as you experience it in the nostrils. Don't follow it down into the chest or abdomen, and don't try to visualise it leaving the body, but keep your attention firmly fixed at the nose.

Relax, but stay alert. In time you will begin to feel the subtle sensation of breath as it enters and leaves the nostrils. Stay with this. When thoughts arise simply notice them. Don't follow them or try to lose them or change them, just be patient and gentle and return the attention to the breath. The same applies to the emotions or sensations in the body. Notice, accept without judgement and return to the breath.

If you must move during the meditation (to scratch an itch for example) use that whole movement as a part of the meditation, not something outside to distract you. Keeping your eyes closed, put your attention in the hand and move slowly to scratch the itch. Feel the weight of the hand, notice any sensations, notice whatever can be noticed. Scratch the itch with awareness, return the hand slowly to your lap and the attention to the breath. Eventually we take this attitude of awareness into our daily life.

Sit in this way for fifteen or twenty minutes and leave the meditation slowly and mindfully, not trying to hold on to a peaceful state of mind, but just being aware, and ready for the next moment of your life.

To practice in this way each day will bring good results. A way of living in the world that is established in balance and wisdom, and the natural ability to accept and then respond to life as it unfolds moment after moment. But remember, consistency is everything. The more we practice the more we receive the results of that practice.

We can extend this simple awareness meditation into the act of walking. Placing our attention on the feet and just noticing the sensations as they change with each step.
The Buddha said that there is only one way to end our experience of unhappiness in the world, and that is the way of awareness.
When we truly understand the real value of awareness training we will want to apply it in every moment and in every situation, from making a cup of tea, to being at our work, from playing with our children to changing channels on the television. From the biggest to the smallest action. Enlightenment waits for us, we only need to be aware to see it.

> Those who follow the Dhamma
> Will reach the Other Shore
> And transcend the realm of death,
> Which is so hard to do.

> Dhammapada: Verse 86

Part Five

Daily Inspirations

The Other Shore

*The one who loves the Dhamma
Will live happily
With his mind at ease.*

Dhammapada: Verse 79

The Other Shore

Daily Inspirations
Changing our life is mostly about remembering to be different.

As we walk this beautiful path of Awareness and Love, letting go patiently and tirelessly of the very causes of our unhappiness, it will be helpful to hear and reflect upon the words of the Buddha and to be reminded of the essence of this teaching.

Here then, are more selected verses from the Dhammapada, to support your effort.

The Dhammapada is part of the Khuddaka Nikaya (shorter discourses) section of the Suttanta Pitaka of the Theravada tradition of Buddhism.

These short verses were given by the Buddha on various occasions during his forty five year ministry, to emphasise and explain different aspects of his teaching and the Dhamma.

For simplicity and economy I have maintained the male gender orientation, and so speak about 'the wise man' and 'he', but this is only a convenience and convention.

Dhamma is equally available to women and men alike, and the only obstacle to true understanding is the mind of the student.

The purpose of Dhamma practice is to go past and transcend all limitations concerning the 'self' identity. Gender is only one more position to take that limits our understanding.

So read, reflect and apply these teachings as best you can in every moment. Allow this beautiful Dhamma to find you and guide you through your life, so that you will be happy, and your very presence will be a blessing to the world.

May you be well and happy.

Verses from the Dhammapada

We are what we think.
All that we are arises from the mind,
And with the mind we make our world.
So, speak or act with an impure mind
And suffering will follow you
As the wheel follows the ox that pulls the cart.

Verse 1

We are what we think.
All that we are arises from the mind,
And with the mind we make our world.
So, speak or act with a pure mind
And happiness will follow you
As your shadow in the brightest part of the day.

Verse 2

Hatred is never overcome by more hatred.
Only Love can overcome hatred -
This is an eternal law.

Verse 5

Many do not realise that one day all will die.
For those who truly realise this truth,
All fighting is ended.

Verse 6

The one who only talks about the teaching
But does not practice,
Is like the cow man who counts the cattle of others.
He has no place in the Sangha.
Verse 19

Meditating earnestly
The wise will realise Nibbana,
The highest happiness.
Verse 23

By sustained effort and self-discipline
The wise man can build himself an island
That no flood can sweep away.
Verse 25

Ignorant and foolish people become lazy.
The wise man regards awareness
As his greatest gift.
Verse 26

The wise man does not look at the faults of others,
Of what they have done or left undone.
The wise man looks only to his own errors.
Verse 50

The wise man will not associate with foolish people,
But will seek friendship with the best of men.

Verse 78

Irrigators guide water,
Fletchers straighten arrows,
Carpenters bend wood,
The wise man shapes himself.

Verse 80

Better than a thousand meaningless words
Is the one word of truth,
That brings peace to the listener.

Verse 100

All men fear pain and death.
All men love life.
Remembering that he is one of them
Let no-one harm or kill another.

Verse 130

It is easy to do that which is harmful to ourselves.
To do that which is good and truly useful is difficult.

Verse 163

By oneself unwholesome actions are made,
And by oneself one suffers.
By oneself wholesome actions are made,
And by oneself one is purified.
Purity and impurity are personal concerns.
No-one can purify another.

Verse 165

Cease to do evil.
Learn to do good.
Purify your own mind.
These are the teachings of all the Buddhas

Verse 183

Let us live happily,
Without hating in return
Those who hate us.
Let us be free from hatred
Amongst those who hate.

Verse 197

Attachment to loved ones
Brings fear and sorrow.
The one who has transcended this attachment
Is free.

Verse 213

The one who always finds fault with others
Will allow his own faults to grow,
And is far, far away from purity.

Verse 253

You yourself must make the effort;
Buddhas only point the way.
Those who have stepped onto the Path
And who meditate,
Will be free from all the ties of delusion.

Verse 276

It is better to be alone
Than with a fool.
Let a wise man walk alone
Like the king elephant in the forest.

Verse 330

The disciple who meditates on Love
And the Dhamma,
Will surely attain Nibbana.

Verse 368

The Other Shore

Acknowlegments

No book ever writes itself, and although the idea always seems simple, the actual work of sharing ones thoughts in a coherent way demands the help of others.
In this respect I feel blessed to have been aided by the people listed below, for their help, support and expertise.

Sayadaw Rewata Dhamma, my late teacher and inspiration in my life.
Isabelle Kewley, my wife, supporter and friend, who typeset the words and designed the cover, thus creating the book you are holding.
Katja Rewerts, friend, supporter and disciple of Dhamma, who as always offered her services to promote Dhamma by reading and correcting the various draughts of this book.
Karin Bartelt, Frank Vaughan and Caroline Farrant, who supported me in many ways.

May you all be well and happy.

The Other Shore

About the author

Michael Kewley is the former Buddhist monk, Paññadipa, and now an internationally acclaimed Master of Dhamma, presenting courses and meditation retreats throughout the world.

A disciple of the late Sayadaw Rewata Dhamma, he teaches solely on the instruction of his own Master, to share the Dhamma, in the spirit of the Buddha, so that all beings might benefit.

Full biography of Michael Kewley can be found at:
www.puredhamma.org

Also by Michael Kewley

HIGHER THAN HAPPINESS
OPENING THE SPIRITUAL HEART
NOT THIS
LIFE CHANGING MAGIC
WALKING THE PATH
LIFE IS NOT PERSONAL
THE REALITY OF KAMMA

The Other Shore

The Other Shore

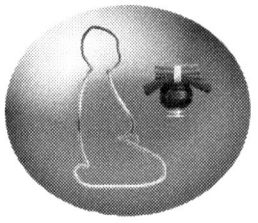

www.puredhamma.org

www.ingramcontent.com/pod-product-compliance
Ingram Content Group UK Ltd.
Pitfield, Milton Keynes, MK11 3LW, UK
UKHW021257180426
11947UKWH00015B/893